Discipline

ALSO BY KEN PARSELL

The Catalyst of Confidence

Discipline

Ken Parsell

Discipline

Email: info@kenparsell.com

Printed in the United States of America

Cover design by Jacqueline Kuschel

ISBN: 978-0615743141
First Edition, February 2013 (Paperback); Re-released March, 2016

To My Wife

Contents

Preface

Discipline is a surprisingly simple thing (hence the little volume you hold). Yet it is something most people dearly struggle with. It requires patience, practice, repetition, consistency, effort. And it seems few of us are able to do what it takes. The struggle continues.

What follows is a model for what has worked in my own life, and I believe if this model is followed consistently it will work for you as well. It is clear that living a good life is closely bound up with being disciplined, and to the extent we are disciplined we are able not merely to live but live well.

There are aspects of this book that may seem repetitive, and this is deliberate, as it mirrors how discipline is developed in practice. I place a special emphasis on the appendix; pay particular attention to what you find there. Become intimate with this book. Highlight it, take notes, re-read it, live it. Like discipline itself, you will get out of it what you put into it.

Ken Parsell
February 29th, 2016

1

Discipline?

"Diets don't work," said the student. The rest of the class seemed somewhat surprised by the statement. We were in the process of discussing self-deception, when, in response to my request for more examples, the off-subject of dieting was introduced. "Why don't they?" I asked. "Because most people can't seem to commit to diets," said the student. "They move from diet to diet, thinking they're making progress, but because they don't sufficiently commit to any of them, they don't end up losing weight—they're deceiving themselves." Obviously such an observation isn't all inclusive and shouldn't properly be attributed to *all* dieters, but even so, the student was right. But why? Is it because diets don't work—period—or is it because people can't seem to commit to them? Is a person's lack of results the fault of the diet, or is it the fault of the person? Before long other students began retorting that they have known people who have lost weight dieting and that some diets do work, provided a person actually follows the plan correctly. This, it seems, is difficult to deny. Assuming no hidden factors are present, if a person fails to lose weight while following a proven diet, it's most likely because they are not actually following it in the first place. They can't seem to commit. And the reason they can't commit is because they lack discipline.

The subject of discipline can be a sensitive one. This is normally due to the fact that, though many people view discipline as something good and desirable, they also tend to view it as something they lack. Consequently, it is often regarded as somewhat unpleasant and menacing to think about, hanging silently over the heads of many like an unwanted specter.

The Lack of Discipline[1]

John wants to save money. But he can never seem to get ahead financially. He has been trying to save for years, but never seems to have any money left over at the end of the month. John has developed the habit of spending his "left over" income on random wants and desires. Over the years he has acquired a lot of "stuff," but has never been able to save. Every now and then he decides to sell some things, but the money he makes from the sale ends up being spent on more stuff. John tells himself that he doesn't make enough money to save and that one day when he is making more money, he will start saving. But John has been telling himself this for years, during which he has received a promotion, and multiple salary increases. Yet John still can't seem to save money.

---

1   Circumstantial profiles like those in this section are offered here and throughout the book as examples or illustrations. If you understand the principles involved and find such examples unnecessary, feel free to skip these sections.

Barb wants to be on time. But she always seems to struggle with being punctual. It doesn't matter where she is going or what she is attending, she is still always late. Of course Barb doesn't *want* to be late. She doesn't plan on being late everywhere she goes. But that's what always seems to happen. In fact, Barb's reputation for being late is so well known that almost everyone she knows expects it from her. And though she often tries to be on time, some urgent, unforeseen problem always pops up at the last minute, delaying her.

Sue wants to stop getting angry at the drop of a hat. If someone says or does something she doesn't approve of, she loses her cool. She swears, yells, throws things. She can't emotionally handle things with which she doesn't agree. If she is at home and her kids do something wrong, she gets needlessly angry. When she is stopped at a traffic light and the car in front of her doesn't immediately go when the light turns green, she honks her horn and shouts obscenities. If she attends a dinner party and someone says something she disagrees with, she doesn't just express her disagreement, she starts a verbal fight. If she and her husband go out to eat and the waitress makes a mistake, she gets upset and insults her. Sue isn't proud of her behavior, and is often deeply regretful after she cools down. She just hasn't been able to figure out how to control herself.

Steve wants to lose 50 pounds. But he gets little daily exercise and has a tendency to overeat and eat unhealthy food. He always feels tired and is sick of having to constantly buy new clothes. When Steve goes on a diet, which he does often, he tends to stray from it. If he happens to be visiting his in-laws and they are having pizza for dinner, he will quickly decide to make an exception. If he doesn't feel like going for a walk, he will resolve to walk *twice* as far the following day to make up for it. But Steve rarely follows through. And though he has been trying to lose weight for years, he hasn't managed to make any progress.

None of these circumstantial-profiles are unfamiliar to us. In fact, most of us would probably agree that such things are fairly common in real life. Still, it should be clear that discipline, or more appropriately, the lack thereof, plays a central role in the plights in which these individuals find themselves. As we have seen, each person outlined is struggling to accomplish something. And the reason they are failing to succeed is because they lack sufficient discipline.

Consequences

A lack of discipline can merit disastrous and often far-reaching consequences. As we have seen, one consequence of a lack of discipline is that it undermines our ability to do things. When we want to accomplish something but we lack discipline, we will often struggle endlessly with little or no results. Why? Because without the discipline needed to do the very thing we are trying to do, it can be almost impossible to actually do it. Despite our best intentions, we will often find ourselves like the examples outlined above, struggling for years to achieve even the most basic goals.

Another consequence of a lack of discipline is that it tends to cause and prolong problems in our life. Consider the problems that could develop for each person outlined above. Let's start with John. If John continues spending his left over income (instead of saving it), what will happen? An obvious answer is that John will never actually save any money. This itself will prevent John from doing certain things. It may, for instance, cause him to lack the needed down-payment for a house or car in the future. Moreover, it may prevent him from being able to retire comfortably. What will result from Barb failing to be on time? She may annoy some of her friends or family. But, on the other hand, should Barb find herself looking for a job in the future, it's possible that her lack of punctuality may prevent her from being seen as a dependable employee. What about Sue? What will happen if she doesn't get a grip on her temper? To start, she will probably damage or destroy quite a few personal relationships and could potentially strain her marriage. Most people don't enjoy being around someone who is always angry. Her job security may be jeopardized; excessive anger and professionalism are rarely compatible. Furthermore, if she takes her anger out on household possessions, it could become quite costly over time. Lastly, what will happen to Steve if he doesn't change his lifestyle and lose weight? Initially, he will have to deal with the consequences of being 50 pounds overweight: feeling tired and regularly buying larger clothes. There may also be physical activities, such as biking or backpacking, that Steve could fully participate in if he wasn't overweight. Additionally, his lack of exercise and healthy eating habits will likely catch up with him in the form of poor health, excessive medical bills, and may even result in premature death.

Discipline and Life

Humanity's general lack of discipline is surely nothing new, but it is still a reality that we ought to consider in our personal and professional lives. After introducing some potential consequences of the lack of discipline, it should hardly be surprising that a lack of discipline is something that undermines our ability to live a good life. Life is inextricably linked with action, and actions are necessarily directed toward some end or goal. But, as we have seen, a lack of discipline frustrates our ability to reach our ends or goals, and also carries the potential to cause and prolong problems in our life. It seems reasonable then, to conclude that discipline is indeed something necessary to live the life we desire, and that to the degree we lack discipline, we also lack the ability to live life to the fullest. If we lack discipline—and we all know if we do—we need to start working to develop it. Before we learn how discipline can be developed, however, let us first determine exactly what discipline is.

2

Discipline & Its Benefits

If you pay attention to how the word discipline is used in everyday conversation, you will quickly notice that, more often than not, it is used to describe something a person *lacks* rather than positively possesses. In other words, people tend to say things like: "I'm just not disciplined" or "I need to be more disciplined" or "so-and-so isn't very disciplined." Discipline is rightly thought to be closely linked with the concepts of "self-control" and "self-mastery." Thus, when someone says something like "I'm not disciplined" or "so-and-so isn't disciplined," what they normally mean is that they, or someone else, lacks self-control or self-mastery in one area or another.

The concepts of self-control and self-mastery presuppose a prescriptive standard of sorts. That is to say that in order to make sense they must reference a standard that *ought* to be followed. Take overeating, for instance. When Steve overeats and later regrets it, perhaps lamenting that he has no self-control, he is presupposing a standard, namely that he believes he should not have overeaten.

Steve concludes the reason he lacks self-control is because he did what he believes he should not have done—he violated the standard. Contrariwise, when Steve actually does what he believes he should do, that is, when he maintains the standard, he can be said to have shown self-control or self-mastery.

We are now in a position to make another observation: Whenever a person evaluates their own level of self-control or self-mastery (or that of another person), they must, along with a prescriptive standard, reference an action or series of actions in relation to that standard. The person that says they lack self-control or self-mastery because they regularly overeat is not only referencing the standard that they ought not overeat, but also that their actions have failed to conform to that standard. Hence, self-control and self-mastery are based on two concepts: 1) a standard that presumably ought to be followed, and 2) the actions of a person in relation to that standard. With these distinctions in mind, we can now begin identifying what discipline is.

Like the prescriptive standard on which the concepts of self-control and self-mastery must be based, discipline presupposes a similar standard: commitment. In order for a person to even be considered a candidate for embodying discipline, they must first consciously commit to do something. By "consciously commit," I mean that they must be aware of a given resolution or commitment—they must be conscious of what they have resolved or committed to do—and they must intend to actually do it. In the same way a prescriptive standard is necessary to measure one's level of self-control or self-mastery, without a consciously formed resolution or commitment, there can be no standard with which to measure discipline against.

Furthermore, just as the concepts of self-control

and self-mastery measure a person's actions in relation to a prescriptive standard, so too does discipline measure a person's actions in relation to what they have committed themselves to do. Notice, as with self-control and self-mastery, we are appealing to two concepts: 1) the consc-ious commitment or resolution made by a person, and 2) a person's actions as they relate to that commitment or resolution. Both are necessary components of discipline.

We can now put forward a simple and under-standable definition of what discipline is. On one hand we must consider what a person *commits* to do, and on the other we must consider what they *actually* do. The first step toward being disciplined is consciously committing to do something. If a person fails to do this, they lack discipline. On the other hand, if a person consciously commits to do something, they must then do the very thing they have committed to do. If they fail to do what they have committed to do, they also lack discipline. In short, if a person either does not make conscious commitments, or if they fail to do the things which they have committed to do, they lack discipline. Thus, discipline is a kind of continuity between one's commitments and one's actions. It is a continuity between that which a person resolves to do, and that which they actually do. Put simply, discipline is doing what one commits to do.

Let us revisit the example of overeating. Suppose Steve has developed the tendency to overeat during meals. Let's say that this isn't something he deliberately decides to do, but rather, is something that just ends up happening. And though this behavior has resulted in his gaining weight and general discomfort, he hasn't yet consciously committed to stop. Now, since Steve hasn't consciously committed to do anything, he can't be said to have discipline in any way. As previously mentioned, discipline presupposes a conscious commitment or resolution. At this point, there is none. But suppose that Steve eventually gets sick of his behavior and consciously commits to change: He resolves to eat a fixed portion at meals. If he does as he has resolved to do, he can be said to be disciplined. And to the extent that he does that which he has resolved to do, he is being disciplined. If, on the other hand, Steve fails to eat a fixed portion, he can be said to lack discipline. And to the extent that he fails to do that which he has resolved to do, he is not being disciplined. Given that Steve has consciously committed to do something, his being disciplined strictly depends upon whether or not he actually does it. If his actions line up with his commitment, he has been disciplined to that extent. If they do not, Steve has, to that extent, failed to be disciplined.

In Summary

Discipline is doing what one commits to do:
- A person *has* discipline if:

    a) they consciously commit to do something, *and:*

    b) they actually do what they have committed to do.
- A person *lacks* discipline if:

    a) they make no conscious commitments, *or:*

    b) they consciously commit to do something, but fail to actually do it.

The Benefits of Discipline

Arguably the greatest benefit to be reaped from developing discipline is an increased ability to accomplish things. If discipline consists in the doing of what we have committed ourselves to do, then, if we are disciplined, it necessarily follows that when we do commit to do something, we are much more likely to act in such a way as to accomplish it. Without any sense of discipline we tend to drift, making few conscious commitments, if any. Every now and then we might think to ourselves: "I need to do this" or "I want to do that." But feeling the need or desire to do something and making a conscious commitment or resolution to do it are not the same thing. If we fail to make conscious commitments, or fail to follow through with the commitments we have made, we put ourselves in a position where we can never accomplish anything except by chance. By developing continuity between our commitments and our actions, we, in short, provide ourselves with the ability to succeed.

Being disciplined also enhances one's level of self-confidence. When we consciously commit to do something, and subsequently do the thing we have committed to do, we validate our ability to act, and ultimately gain an increased understanding of ourselves. The more disciplined a person is the more confidence they tend to have in their own abilities. And since disciplined people only commit to do things they intend to do, it never occurs to them to doubt their ability to make good on their commitments. Ultimately, this cycle of behavior leads to an increased confidence in oneself.

Another benefit to be had from developing discipline is that people are much more likely to trust you. As mentioned, disciplined people have a tendency to only commit to something if they know they will follow through with it. In other words, what they "say they will do" and what they "actually do" line up. They are consistent in their words (commitments) and in their deeds (actions). Such behavior is naturally trustworthy. And since trust is essentially the "glue" that holds all meaningful relationships together, this is definitely an added benefit.

It is still worth mentioning that discipline also helps eliminate or prevent the problems that can result from indiscipline. As we saw in the circumstantial-profiles outlined in Chapter 1, the lack of discipline can, depending on the circumstances, result in a multiplicity of short-term and long-term consequences. But such consequences, insofar as they arise from a lack of discipline, cannot persist when a person is disciplined.

Lastly, developing discipline enables a person to more fully realize their potential. As we have said, life is inextricably linked with purposeful behavior (action). And the better equipped we are to act in such a way that enables us to achieve the things we are capable of, the better equipped we are to live the life we desire. As stated in Chapter 1, our ability to live a good life is ultimately dependent on the degree to which we develop discipline.

3

How to Develop Discipline

Up to this point we have considered discipline as the ability to do what one commits to do. We have explored some of the benefits of developing discipline in our personal lives, as well as some of the potential hazards that can result from indiscipline. Notwithstanding the obvious benefits of discipline, its widespread deficiency is hard to deny.

It is important to note that discipline itself is a skill. It is not something that we are born with or possess naturally because we are human. Rather, it is something that we must develop and cultivate by virtue of our own actions and behavior. As such, discipline is some-thing that develops over time. It requires consistent effort, focus and practice. But it is something that can be developed by anyone, provided they are willing to learn and work at it.

Analyzing our actions and behavior is the key to understanding how we can develop discipline. When we say a person is disciplined, we don't mean that "once upon a time" they committed to do something and actually did it. On the contrary, we mean that such a person tends to do what they commit to do on a regular or consistent basis. They act a certain way—consistently—over time. By the same token, when we say a person lacks discipline, we don't mean that on some rare occasion they failed to do what they committed to do, but rather, that they consistently fail to do what they commit to do. When we act a certain way consistently over time, we develop behavioral patterns or habits—our actions perpetuate themselves—and before long we are able to perform such actions without consciously thinking about it. In his 1926 book *The Story of Philosophy*, Will Durant states, paraphrasing the Greek philosopher Aristotle: "Excellence is an art won by training and habituation. We do not act rightly because we have virtue or excellence, but we rather have those because we have acted rightly." Just as excellence begets excellence, so too does discipline beget discipline, and indiscipline, indiscipline. In light of this comparison, it may be helpful to reformulate Durant's summation: "Discipline is an art won by training and habituation. We do not act with discipline because we have discipline, but we rather have discipline because we have acted with discipline." Thus, we can develop discipline by acting with discipline. How, then, can we act with discipline?

If you recall, in the last chapter it was stated that discipline is based on two concepts: 1) consciously committing to do something, and 2) actually doing it. If we want to develop discipline, these concepts provide us with the blueprint—they show us what it means to act with discipline. The person who consciously commits to do something, and actually does it, is acting in such a way as to develop discipline—they are acting with discipline. Whereas the person who fails to consciously commit to do something, or fails to actually do what they commit to do, is acting in such a way as to develop indiscipline. And in the sense that they are not acting in a way conducive to developing discipline—they are not acting with discipline. Furthermore, it is not enough to simply "act with discipline" every now and then (as considered above). If we truly want to develop discipline, we must develop the *habit* of acting with discipline. We must acquire discipline through a kind of training and habituation, i.e., we must consistently do the things we consciously commit to do.

In order to develop discipline, you must practice two things:

1) Making conscious commitments.
2) Doing everything you consciously commit to do.

Practice #1: Making Conscious Commitments

A conscious commitment is a decision or resolution made by a person that he or she fully intends to do. Without them, we have no standard to measure our subsequent actions against, and as a result we cannot possibly be disciplined. If we lack discipline, conscious commitments provide us with a clear starting point to develop it. As stated above, the first thing you must do to begin developing discipline is practice making conscious commitments. To do this, the following suggestions should be helpful:

a) Be aware of what you commit to do.
b) Be specific and detailed.
c) Only commit to do something if you are absolutely sure you will do it.
d) Start with small things.
e) Start with few things.

a) Be aware of what you commit to do: Many of us have developed the tendency to drift along when it comes to making decisions, not being fully aware of the process involved. Occasionally something might snap us out of our psychological negligence, but for the most part we rely on a kind of autopilot to govern many (if not most) of our decisions and commitments. Start working to develop an in-the-moment awareness of your decisions. Try to stop yourself when you are about to make a choice and think about what it is you are doing. Pay attention to how you approach things psychologically and begin making conscious commitments. The act of making conscious commitments will itself help you develop an understanding of what goes on in your mind when you make a decision. Over time, stop or minimize your psychological autopilot and try to be fully aware of the things you commit yourself to do.

b) Be specific and detailed: When you make a conscious commitment, be specific. Avoid generalizing what it is you intend to do. To illustrate, let's briefly return to Steve's struggle with overeating. Recall his conscious commitment was not a commitment to "stop overeating" or to "lose weight," each of which is horribly general and lacking in detail. Steve's conscious commitment was rather to "eat a fixed portion at meals." When your conscious commitments are specific and detailed, you provide yourself with an exact standard of behavior; you know specifically what needs to be done. Moreover, because your commitment is specific and detailed, you will always know whether or not you actually did it.

c) Only commit to do something if you are absolutely sure you will do it: If you have any doubt whatsoever about whether or not you will do something, do not commit yourself to do it. Before you commit to do something, think about it. Ask yourself: "Do I really intend to do this?" "Will I do this?" It is easy to begin making conscious commitments, but never forget that your goal is to develop discipline, which requires that you actually do the things that you consciously commit to do. It's easy to be overzealous with commitments, but it is better to commit *not* to do something (and follow through on not doing it), rather than failing to do something that you have committed yourself to do. (Note: If you commit yourself *not to do something*, and you in fact don't do it, you are still exercising discipline.)

d) Start with small things: It is of no benefit to consciously commit to do something if you don't end up doing it. Remember, your goal is to develop discipline, not suddenly be perfect. One of the best ways to begin developing discipline is to start consciously committing to small things. Consciously commit to get dressed in the morning. Consciously commit to eat breakfast, lunch, and dinner, and do so daily. Consciously commit to take out the trash or get the mail. And follow through on each of your commitments. This alone will affect you tremendously. Not only will you begin developing the habit of doing the things you have committed to do (regardless how small they may be), you will also gain an increased awareness of your decision-making process. As time goes on, you will feel more comfortable committing to do bigger and bigger things. The habit of being disciplined in the little things will invariably begin "flowing over" into bigger and bigger things. Thus, discipline can be developed over time by committing to and following through on baby steps. If you commit yourself to do something too big, you will likely fail to follow through on it, thereby undermining the process of developing discipline.

e) Start with few things: Just as it's a good idea to

begin developing discipline by committing to small things (as stated above), it is also beneficial to begin by committing to few things. Be picky with your conscious commitments, especially when you first begin. Avoid committing to do too many things at once. It's easy to get excited at the prospect of being disciplined, but never forget that the goal of committing to do something is actually doing it. By guarding yourself against the temptation of committing to do too much too soon, you help pave the way for the early success that is crucial to developing discipline as a habit.

Practice #2: Doing Everything You Consciously Commit to Do

While conscious commitments provide us with the starting point to develop discipline, they do not solely determine whether or not we are disciplined. It is still possible for us to consciously commit to do something, yet not actually do it. If we want to be disciplined, we still have to act. If we make a conscious commitment to do something, we must still do the thing we have committed ourselves to do. This is pretty straight forward, but is often easier said than done. The following suggestions should be helpful:

a) Support your commitments with immediate action.
b) If necessary, divide your actions into small steps.

a) Support your commitments with immediate action: The word immediate should be understood as "as soon as possible." The idea here is to develop the habit of supporting your decisions and commitments with action.

The best way to do this is to get into action as soon as you can. The longer you delay action, the more difficult it can be to get started and actually do whatever it is you have committed to do. If you commit to exercise on Mondays, Wednesdays, and Fridays, for instance, you should do so as soon as you possibly can on those days. Unless, of course, you have committed to a specific time of day. In any case, the longer you delay or postpone action, the easier it is to give up and fall back into habits of indiscipline.

  b) If necessary, divide your actions into small steps: Although this suggestion is very similar to the aforementioned "start with small things," there is one major difference: Start with small things focuses on conscious commitments themselves, whereas this suggestion is concerned with the actions necessary to accomplish a given commitment. Some commitments are an "all or nothing" deal. Such as getting out of bed when your alarm goes off: either you do or you don't. But depending on your individual temperament, and depending on the commitment itself, it may be advantageous to "split up" the actions necessary to accomplish it. For instance, suppose you commit to read 30 minutes every day. By splitting the allocated amount of time into parts (say, three ten minute steps, or two fifteen minute steps), you can provide yourself with a series of "stepping stones" that can help you successfully follow through on your commitment. (Note: Another, perhaps simpler option, would be to lower the commitment to a *single* ten or fifteen minute daily reading session, and slowly increase it over time.)

In Summary

If you lack discipline, start committing to do specifically defined small things. Only commit to do things that you know you will actually do. Again, it makes no difference how small a given commitment happens to be, what matters is that you have consciously committed to do it, and that you follow through on it. Remember: You are working to develop the habit of doing what you commit to do. For large things, consciously commit not to commit to them. As you begin making good on your initial commitments, you will begin to realize that you can steadily increase the size and scope of your commitments. Again, only commit to do things that you fully intend to do, and slowly and incrementally increase the size and scope of your resolutions. Remember: It's better to commit *not* to do something (and follow through on not doing it), than it is to fail to do something that you have committed yourself to do. Over time, as you continue practicing making conscious commitments and doing the things you consciously commit to do (acting with discipline), you will begin developing discipline as a habit. And the more consistent your disciplined actions are, the stronger and more seamless your "habit of disciplined behavior" will become. Eventually, you will develop discipline to such an extent that it becomes part of who you are, which should be your ultimate goal: to develop such a thoroughgoing discipline that it becomes automatic—a way of life.

In addition, practicing these steps consistently over time will increase your general awareness of both your commitments and your actions; it will raise your level of self-understanding and will enable you to make more accurate decisions and resolutions in the future. It will enable you to start acting deliberately and "on purpose," as opposed to acting on the basis of a kind of psychological autopilot. The former helps you live deliberately and reinforces your ability to be disciplined. The latter causes you to drift and sabotages your ability to act effectively. In the end, the level of your awareness of yourself and your behavior will determine the extent to which you can develop discipline.

Illustrations

To further illustrate how discipline can be developed, let us revisit the circumstantial-profiles outlined in Chapter 1.

John feels that he should save money, but ends up rationalizing his way out of it, opting instead to spend his discretionary income on "stuff." Knowing this, John should make a conscious commitment to save money, deciding on a set amount per paycheck. Utilizing the suggestion to "start with small things," he should initially commit to a relatively low dollar amount, such as $20 per paycheck. If he is unsure whether or not he can deposit $20 per paycheck in savings, he should reduce the dollar amount further. Even if he only ends up committing to save $5 per paycheck, he has still committed to a specific and detailed amount, and, provided he in fact follows through consistently on his $5 commitment, he is slowly developing discipline as a habit. After a few paychecks and consistent $5 deposits into savings, he should then begin to slowly increase the amount. Let's say that after observing how simple it is to save such a small amount of money, John will probably realize that $20 per paycheck isn't so bad after all. However, John should take care to be sure that he will actually make good on his $20 commitment before he consciously commits to it. If he "bites off more than he can chew," so to speak, his efforts will backfire, and he will once again fall back into old habits. After making good on his $20 commitment for a few weeks or months, he should once again feel comfortable enough to increase the amount, again, taking care to not over-commit himself. As John's savings account increases in value, so too will his belief and confidence in his ability to save. And after years of saving, his financial life will change dramatically.

Barb feels that she should be on time, but isn't. She may not necessarily know what goes wrong, but for some reason she always seems to end up running late. Before deciding to consciously commit to being punctual, however, it may be best for Barb first to commit to some smaller things. The reason being that committing to being on time may be too much for her to handle at first. Again, the idea is to slowly build up one's level of discipline over time, rather than doing it all at once. The latter approach often proves to be too difficult and thus results in frustration and indiscipline. After committing to do some rather menial things, such as getting dressed in the morning or brushing her teeth—and consistently following through on such things—Barb should then commit to be on time for a single thing. Using the suggestion "Be specific and detailed" she should determine exactly how long it will take her to get where she is going, and then determine what time she needs to leave her house. Barb's commitment should be something like "I will pull out of my driveway at 8:35 A.M." If Barb does as she has committed herself to do, she can be said to be disciplined in that endeavor. She should then commit to be on time for another event, again determining exactly when she should leave, and again, following through on her commitment. If Barb can continue committing herself to leave at a specific time, and can continue making good on her commitments, she will slowly develop the habit of being punctual.

If you recall, Sue has a tendency to get angry over pretty much anything. Often regretting her behavior after the fury of her emotions have subsided, she knows that she needs to change. But Sue's situation is a little different from the others. She is dealing with emotional reactions, which can be very unpredictable and hard to pin down. In order for Sue to stop getting angry, she needs to decide on an alternative behavior to replace getting angry. Suppose she decides that instead of getting angry she will focus on her breathing: "breathe in, breathe out." In this way, she can begin learning to control her emotional reactions. Next Sue should begin by cultivating discipline with some "small commitments." By initially committing to some small things—like running on the treadmill for ten minutes or washing the car once a week—she will slowly begin increasing her level of self-awareness. She should then choose a specific "trigger" that is likely to cause her to get angry, and commit to "focus on her breathing" the next time that particular trigger occurs. Her increased awareness of her commitments and actions should help her detect the next time she feels compelled to get angry, at which point she needs to "focus on her breathing." By doing this over and over, and slowly committing to conquer more of her emotional triggers, Sue will steadily develop the ability to control how she responds to her emotions.

Despite being a compulsive dieter, Steve, like many people, has been trying to lose weight for years. The first thing Steve should do is commit to temporarily stop dieting. At this point his so called "commitment" to a diet means absolutely nothing, because he doesn't follow through on his commitment. Before Steve can effectively commit to a diet, he must first develop discipline. Thus, Steve should begin by consciously committing to do some unrelated "small things." He can consciously commit to mow the lawn, fix some things around the house, take a shower, or even make a sandwich. Again, what is important is that he is developing the habit of being disciplined, albeit in small and seemingly insignificant ways. As Steve develops the habit of making conscious commitments and following through on them, he will gain an increased awareness of his decisions and actions, and will find himself able to commit to bigger and bigger things. But Steve should not commit to a diet all at once. Rather, after determining which diet he would like to pursue, he should begin by committing to small parts of it, one at a time. Over time, Steve will feel more comfortable committing to additional aspects of the diet, which he should do, but only if he is absolutely sure that he will follow through on them. Eventually, he will be in a position to successfully commit to the entire diet.

Stumbling Blocks

As you begin working to develop discipline, you will likely encounter some difficulties. This is a normal part of the process, and you should not allow yourself to be discouraged by it. Remember, you are working to change your habits, and that is not something that happens overnight. Habits are hard to change, but once changed they are maintained with far less effort. Though there are many potential stumbling blocks to developing discipline, they can be divided in two categories:

    a) Drifting
    b) Inconsistency

a) Drifting: Our minds are constantly engaged in a battle between conscious and unconscious action. Practicing the steps necessary to develop discipline helps direct our minds toward conscious and deliberate action. As discussed, the consistent and repeated practice of 1) making conscious commitments, and 2) doing everything we consciously commit to do, results in an increased awareness of a) our decisions and commitments, and b) the actions which correspond to them. As we continue developing discipline, our self-awareness increases. However, we must always be on guard against falling back to the unconscious side of things (losing our self-awareness), which I refer to as drifting. Drifting occurs when we stop being conscious of what is going on, i.e., we stop being fully aware of our commitments and our actions which correspond to them. We simply drift along. This inevitably leads to a breakdown in disciplined behavior. Without the awareness of our decisions and commitments, and the actions which correspond to them, we act unconsciously, that is, on the basis of a kind of psychological autopilot. On the other hand, when we are aware of our decisions and commitments, and the actions which correspond to them, we act deliberately and "on purpose."

It's easy to fall into the pattern of drifting when we first begin trying to develop discipline. Symptoms of drifting may include failing to make conscious commitments, having a hard time remembering things you have committed to do, or even struggling to remember to follow through on commitments you have made. If you're having trouble making conscious commitments, revisit the above section on Making Conscious Commitments, and start working to develop new habits. If you tend to forget to make commitments, or forget your commitments after you make them, or forget to follow through on them, you need to develop a system to remind yourself to do so.

Forgetfulness is probably the most common form of drifting. Until we develop the habit of doing something consistently, we will be doing something that we are un-accustomed to. And actions we are unaccustomed to are easily forgotten. Generally speaking, the reason we forget to do something new is because we do not "keep it before us," we don't stay focused on our objectives. If I have made a new commitment to read every day, for instance, but I constantly forget to do so, then I need to develop a way of keeping such a commitment before me, that is, fresh and focused in my conscious mind. How can I do this? The possibilities here are almost endless: Written messages, sticky notes, online calenders, email, cellphone, alarms, etc., physical objects set in view that can represent various things like commitments, tying a string around your finger to remind yourself, and so on. The key is to develop a system, through trial and error, that effectively serves the purpose of reminding you to do something, whatever it is that "something" may be. After you have reminded yourself often enough, consistently over time, and subsequently done whatever it was you reminded yourself to do, you will slowly begin developing the habit of staying focused and minimizing forgetfulness, which ultimately helps minimize drifting.

b) Inconsistency: There are times when you will commit to do something and fail to actually do it, and to that extent you are being inconsistent, i.e., you commit to do one thing, but end up doing something else. Incon-sistency is a problem because it undermines discipline. Indeed, such behavior is contrary to discipline. If you con-tinue being inconsistent, over time you will soon develop inconsistency as a habit, which can dramatically under-mine your ability to accomplish things.

No one is perfect. Even the most disciplined person will fail to make good on a commitment at some point. The key to becoming disciplined is simply doing what you commit to do significantly more often than not. When you are working to develop new habits—habits of disciplined behavior—you will inevitably fail at some point. Developing discipline takes time, and it takes persistence. If you fail, it's not the end of the world. But if you begin failing consistently (being consistently inconsistent) you should stop and analyze what is going on. To be sure, being consciously aware of your failure is actually a good thing, because it shows you are conscious of what is going on. Developing discipline is largely a matter of self-awareness, a matter of deliberate and conscious action. Hence, your awareness of your failures is most certainly a good thing: when you are consciously aware that you are acting inconsistently, you can consciously change your actions. Had you never realized your failure, you would be in a far worse situation.

If you notice that you are being inconsistent (committing to do something, but not actually doing it), then you are probably committing to do something "too big," and should temporarily stop committing to do it (or commit not to do it), or redefine the size of the commitment. For instance, because Steve wants to lose weight but lacks discipline, it's probably a bad idea for him to change his entire diet all at once. Concentrating on committing to various aspects of a diet, one at a time, and allowing the commitments to build up as time passes, is probably a better alternative. If Steve commits to do too much too soon, he's likely to fail and get discouraged. If that happens, Steve should concentrate on dialing back his commitments and only commit to do something if he is absolutely sure he will do it. He needs to develop the habit of doing what he commits to do, no matter how small the commitment is. Over time, Steve can begin committing to bigger and bigger things, but only if he is sure he will follow though.

4

Final Thoughts

Developing discipline is part of our potential as human beings. With it, we posses the ability to live a good, whole, complete, and truly human life. Without it, we sink to the level of beasts. Though discipline is largely held to be a virtue that exists beyond the reach of the majority, it is nonetheless within reach of the average person, provided they are willing to learn, work hard, and persist through their failures. In Chapter 3 we reformulated the Aristotelian words of Will Durant: "Discipline is an art won by training and habituation. We do not act with discipline because we have discipline, but we rather have discipline because we have acted with discipline." By acting with discipline—by consciously committing to do something and subsequently doing it, consistently over time—anyone can develop discipline.

On your journey to develop discipline, there may be times when you are deeply discouraged. Never forget that developing discipline is a process, a process that takes time and patience. Remember that your awareness of your failures is the first step to correcting them. And always remember that no one is perfect. Even the most disciplined people fail to make good on their commitments from time to time. The key to being disciplined is simply doing what you commit to do significantly more often than not. If you can do that, you'll know that you can do just about anything to which you put your mind.

Appendix: A

Exercises In Discipline

Just as muscles are maintained and strengthened by physical exercise, so too can we maintain and strengthen our level of discipline by a kind of exercise. This technique, if practiced consistently, will help you further develop and strengthen your level of discipline as well as increase your self-awareness. It consists of practicing deliberate disciplined behavior by doing one (or both) of the following:

1) Give up something you like (for a limited time or single occasion).

2) Do something that you normally wouldn't do (for a limited time or single occasion).

1) Give up something you like: As medieval as it sounds, you would be surprised at how much such a thing can help you maintain discipline. There are two guidelines: Whatever you give up must be a) something you like, and b) a fairly regular part of your life. As an example, suppose I love popcorn and consume it on a regular basis.

As we can see, eating popcorn meets our basic criteria: It is a) something I like, and is b) a regular part of my life. Since it qualifies as something I can give up, let's say I decide to give it up. The first thing I must do is consciously commit to give up eating popcorn for a specific amount of time, say one week. Upon committing to avoid popcorn for one week, I must then do what I have committed to do: I must avoid popcorn for the duration of the week. After which, I can resume eating my beloved popcorn.

2) Do something that you normally wouldn't do: Suppose I generally sleep-in on Saturdays. I usually wouldn't get up at 7:00 A.M. that day, so doing so would indeed qualify as doing something that I normally wouldn't do. Or suppose that I rarely cook. Committing to prepare a meal on a given day would also qualify as something that I normally wouldn't do. In any case, regardless of what I choose to do—as long as I consciously commit to do it, and subsequently do the thing to which I have committed —I have completed a basic "exercise in discipline."

By occasionally (at least once a month) giving up something you like, or by doing something that you normally wouldn't do, you deliberately practice a form of disciplined behavior. This serves to keep you consciously aware of your general and everyday decisions and commitments, and the actions which correspond to them. It reinforces an "I control my actions" paradigm, which helps to mentally keep you on the side of deliberate and purposeful action and prevents you from operating on the basis of psychological autopilot. In short, exercises in discipline help you strengthen your general level of discipline, which in turn provides you with a kind of "reserve" to call upon when you need to exercise discipline and self-control in the future.

In *The Principles of Psychology*, William James gives us a brilliant example of what I am here calling Exercises in Discipline; it is worth quoting at length:

Keep the faculty of effort alive in you by a little gratuitous exercise every day. That is, be systematically heroic in little unnecessary points, do every day or two something for no other reason than its difficulty, so that, when the hour of dire need draws nigh, it may find you not unnerved and untrained to stand the test. Asceticism of this sort is like the insurance which a man pays on his house and goods. The tax does him no good at the time, and possibly may never bring him a return. But, if the fire does come, his having paid it will be his salvation from ruin. So with the man who has daily inured himself to habits of concentrated attention, energetic volition, and self-denial in unnecessary things. He will stand like a tower when everything rocks around him, and his softer fellow-mortals are winnowed like chaff in the blast.

We are spinning our own fates, good or evil, and never to be undone. Every smallest stroke of virtue or of vice leaves its never-so-little scar. The drunken Rip Van Winkle, in Jefferson's play, excuses himself for every fresh dereliction by saying, "I won't count this time!" Well, he may not count it, and a kind Heaven may not count it; but it is being counted none the less. Down among his nerve-cells and fibres the molecules are counting it, registering and storing it up to be used against him when the next temptation comes.

Appendix: B

Common Questions

Q: How long does it take to develop the habit of acting with discipline?

A: Normally somewhere between three weeks and one month, though it could possibly take longer. When we begin acting with discipline, we generally pick out a set of things that we want to be disciplined about. Things like saving money, following a fixed diet, and so on. Each area that we want to be disciplined in involves a certain series of actions, and when we develop discipline in these areas we will inevitably perform the same series of approximate actions over and over again (for each area). Over time our behavior falls into a fixed pattern—a disciplined routine— eventually becoming habitual. Again, it normally takes somewhere from three weeks to one month for a new action (or set of actions) to become a habit. And the longer we maintain a habit, the closer to second nature it will become. For tips on developing discipline "in general," see "Exercises In Discipline" from Appendix: A (p. 41).

Q: Is it always hard to develop discipline in a given area?

A: It isn't *always* hard, but it usually is, mainly because we are doing something new, that is, something to which we are unaccustomed. As with any new activity, the early stages are the most difficult, but as the days and weeks pass it gradually gets easier, until eventually we become accustomed to our new activity. After months or years of consistently acting with discipline in a given area (like saving money or following a fixed diet or whatever), the habit of acting with discipline in that area becomes an integral part of our lifestyle. And at that point the habit of acting with discipline in that area will likely be, ironically, hard to break.

Q: Is it ever permissible to break a commitment? If so, at what point can a commitment be broken?

A: Of course you can break commitments, it's just not going to to help you develop discipline. Indeed, such behavior will undermine your ability to develop discipline because it leads to the habit of indiscipline. Still, the answer is yes, there are circumstances where breaking a commitment is permissible. For example, suppose you commit to run five miles tomorrow after work. But when the time comes, it's pouring rain. If we assume that you don't happen to be a "pouring rain" kind of runner, then something external—that is, something outside of your control—has prevented you from keeping your commit-ment. If something beyond your control prevents you from keeping a given commitment, it's not a big deal. In fact in terms of developing discipline, it isn't a problem at all. The problem arises when you *yourself* are the cause of your failing to keep a commitment. Having said as much, it is important to remember not to make *excuses* in order to avoid a commitment. Return to the running example: if you decide not to run because you "don't feel like it" or because you think it "looks like it might possibly rain," then you are cheating yourself out of your ability to develop discipline.

Q: You suggest that a person should first commit to "small things" and then slowly increase the "size and scope" of their commitments. How do I know when I am ready for a "larger" commitment?

A: Small commitments are easy to commit to, mostly because we know that we will follow through on them. When we consistently follow through on small commitments, we gain a certain amount of self-awareness and confidence in our abilities, which in turn, confirms our ability to act and be disciplined. This understanding allows us to know whether or not we are ready to increase the "size" of a commitment. In other words we should feel confident in our ability to make good on a given "larger" commitment. A good rule to follow when you want to increase a commitment is to is ask yourself: "If I increase my commitment to x, do I feel confident that I will actually do it?"

Q: What should I do about "all or nothing" commitments —those that can't be broken down into smaller commitments?

A: For contrast purposes, let's begin with an example that *can* be broken down into smaller commitments: dieting. Any diet can be broken down into smaller "steps." If a person wants to commit to a "no carb" diet, for example, they could begin by avoiding carbohydrates for breakfast only. Later they could commit to avoid them for breakfast and lunch, and so on, until over time they can commit to the entire diet. Now, as you say, "all or nothing" commitments do exist. (They are rare, however. Most of the time a person just hasn't thought carefully enough about how they can break a commitment down into smaller steps.) An example of this would be getting out of bed when your alarm goes off. Of course it's possible to "prep" yourself by promptly responding to an alarm during the day, or even getting out of bed when your alarm goes off after you have already slept in. And such things may help lay the groundwork for developing the habit of responding immediately to an alarm clock. But an alarm clock itself is usually indicative of an early morning, and you can't ease yourself into being shocked out of your sleep at 5:00 a.m. (or whenever), and subsequently responding with immediate action (getting out of bed). Such a situation calls for you to "bite the bullet," which could be extremely difficult at first. Over time, however, if you continue acting with discipline (in this case, if you continue getting out of bed when your alarm clock goes off), you will eventually (usually it takes three weeks to one month) become accustomed to such behavior.

If you have a question you would like to ask please email the author at info@kenparsell.com.

Appendix: C

Some Thoughts on Habit

Discipline is the result of habit. In this little book I drew upon a theory of habit which up to this point has not been explicitly articulated. Although a sense of what I take habit to be can be gleaned from the foregoing pages, it would no doubt be desirable to some and helpful to others if I were to shed some light on the subject.

I have written about habit in *The Catalyst of Confidence*. But I now believe my treatment there was in many ways was too simplistic and undeveloped. Indeed my understanding of habit has broadened and deepened. In *The Catalyst of Confidence* I defined habit as mere "subconscious action." When we do something repeatedly over time we develop the habit of doing it, "habit" being that part of us that does things automatically. Through repetition we become accustomed to a given action or set of actions until eventually we can perform without conscious thought. There is no need to think about how to tie your shoe, you just do it, i.e., you have tied your shoe enough times that the activity now requires no conscious effort. Such activity is a habit. The same can be said for almost everything we do, and because the things we do have effects—that is, because they produce results—they have a positive or negative impact on our lives. It is therefore our responsibility to create habits which produce positive rather than negative results.

This account of habit is incomplete. It isn't necessarily false. It's just not the whole story, it's too narrow. It does conform to our experience up to a point, but it cannot account for the relationship between habit and voluntary choices.[2] Habit as described above refers to what I would now qualify as "behavioral habits" or habits of unconscious action. Putting your pants on the same way every day can indeed be described as a habit, but only in a restricted behavioral sense. A proper definition of habit requires something more general than "subconscious action" can allow.

The definition of habit I have settled upon is as follows. Habit is a formed disposition to act. It is to be disposed or inclined to act a certain way. It is the tending or orientation of certain actions. I say formed disposition to act, because although there are similarities, habit and instinct are not the same.[3] Habits—dispositions to act—are not innate, they are the result of something done, they are the retained effect of something experienced—specifically

---

2 It was part of my original understanding of habit that any action, mental or physical, if repeated often and over time, would eventually lead to the subconscious performing of said actions. But this understanding leads to problems if the actions in question are volitional. For instance, on this view if I make a deliberate choice to do what is demanded by justice (such as returning money to a cashier who had given me too much change), and do so enough times, I will eventually begin making such choices without any conscious awareness of them—a conclusion which in no way corresponds to our experience.

3 Instincts refer to innate tendencies.

the experience of repeated choices or actions. Habits are not original nature, they are second nature. The expression "habit is second nature" is ancient, and has been referenced by philosophers over millennia from Aristotle to Cicero, from Hegel to James. What is meant by it is that our innate tendencies, those we have by nature, have within them a potency which can be further developed and honed. That we as humans can fashion a second nature which, although ultimately rooted in the first, in many ways surpasses, trumps, and triumphs over it. Habits are formed, and can be formed deliberately.

Beneath this umbrella of habit two distinctions can be made: The distinction between what I am calling behavioral and volitional habits. Behavioral habits are those habits which were described above, those habits formed mostly from repeated physical activity which have since become automatic and now nearly or completely lack conscious awareness. Behavioral habits are indeed important and have their place, in fact we need them in order to survive.[4] But it is the other kind of habit— volitional habit—which carries the greater weight, and is the more important of the two. Volitional habits are habits which we have created from the repetition of choices. The word "choice" may be misleading, however. What I have in mind is specifically volitional choices, conscious decisions, deliberate actions, acts of will, etc. So while behavioral habits are responsible for the particulars of our physical behavior and tendencies, such physical movement

---

4 Imagine having to consciously think about how to tie your shoes each time you tie them. What would it be like to to have to focus on the mechanics of raising food to your mouth each time you eat? If much of our behavior were not taken over by a kind of subconscious automatism, what increased drudgery and effort life would require! This is why in *The Principles of Psychology*, William James refers to habit as "the flywheel of society."

as the way we walk, talk, laugh, cry, express emotions, respond to criticism, compliments, anger, and so on, volitional habits are responsible for our character as human beings. To possess a volitional habit is to dispose one's will toward a given end. The deliberate choosing to lie, for instance, will result, if repeated, in the disposition or propensity to lie, just as consistently choosing to be honest results in a disposition towards honesty.[5] John Stuart Mill speaks of what I call volitional habits when he speaks of habit as a "completely fashioned will." A person's character can thus be understood as a kind of sum total of their developed habits or dispositions to act.

At this point it should be clear why volitional habits are more important than behavioral habits. Being responsible for our character, indeed constituting our character, volitional habits have a direct bearing on how well we live our lives, which is why Aristotle stresses the importance of forming good habits in youth. But what exactly are good habits?

In its most general sense the word "good" signifies the desirable: that which we desire is perceived by us as being good in some way. But although we always act for the good, in the sense that we always do what we think is in some way good, we need to develop the discernment necessary to differentiate what is really good from what merely appears to be good. The real good is what is actually good for us, the apparent good is what we think is good for us in the moment, and it is the real good which ought to be the end and purpose of our actions and choices, and thus our habits. Just as Steve from the circu-

---

5 We lie or tell the truth because we have developed the habit of doing so. Our character can only be described as such because we have developed it from habit, which itself derives and is formed from individual actions and choices.

mstantial profiles struggles with overeating, when he overeats he does so because he desires to. But his desire in this case is for an apparent good, and not a real good. And this is not merely someone's opinion, as overeating and continuous weight gain will affect objective aspects of Steve's life which are real goods—such as health, wealth, longevity, personal time, time with family and friends, and so forth. To be sure, knowing the difference between real and apparent good is not always easy or clear, and to a great extent we must learn from experience and hindsight. Nonetheless, it is the real good and not merely apparent good that we seek, and it is with this in mind that we must act and choose and thus shape our habits and character.

Acknowledgments

I would be remiss to fail to acknowledge those who have been integral to the completion of this project: my wife Cindy, who believes in me more than I deserve; my great friend, Michael "Ollie" Wiitala, whose analysis and thought I value highly; and my "page-cutting, sentence-hacking, redundancy-eliminating, eye-for-detail" editor/ designer, Jacqueline Kuschel. My sincere and humble thanks to each one of you.

Sources

Adler, Mortimer J. *Six Great Ideas*. New York: Touchstone, 1997.

Adler, Mortimer J. *The Great Ideas*. New York: Macmillan Publishing Company, 1990.

Aristotle. *The Basic Works of Aristotle*. New York: Random House, 2001.

Bradberry, Travis and Greaves, Jean. *The Emotional Intelligence Quick Book*. New York: Simon & Schuster, 2005.

Bradberry, Travis and Greaves, Jean. *Emotional Intelligence 2.0*. San Diego: TalentSmart, 2009.

Dyer, Wayne W. *Your Erroneous Zones*. New York: HarperCollins, 1993.

Hill, Napoleon and Lechter, Sharon. *Outwitting the Devil*. New York: Sterling, 2011.

Hill, Napoleon. *The Master-Key to Riches*. New York: Random House, 1965.

Hill, Napoleon. *Think and Grow Rich*. New York: Random House, 1937.

Maltz, Maxwell. *Psycho-Cybernetics*. New York: Simon & Schuster, 1960.

Parsell, Ken. *The Catalyst of Confidence: A Simple and Practical Guide to Understanding Human Potential*. Brighton: Parsell Enterprise Group, 2011.

Stone, W. Clement. *Believe and Achieve*. Wise: The Napoleon Hill Foundation, 1991.

Waitley, Denis. *The Psychology of Winning*. New York: Berkley Publishing Group, 1979.

Ken Parsell is a writer and philomath. His primary research interests are philosophy, psychology, economics, and history. He is the author of *The Catalyst of Confidence* and *Discipline*. Ken lives in Michigan with his family.

Visit his website at
www.kenparsell.com

www.ingramcontent.com/pod-product-compliance
Lightning Source LLC
Chambersburg PA
CBHW060538030426
42337CB00021B/4332